D0559186

AFRICAN-AMERICAN FACTS

MARCUS WILLIAMSON

GRAMERCY BOOKS
NEW YORK

This 2000 edition is published by Gramercy Books™,an imprint of Random House Value Publishing, Inc.,280 Park Avenue, New York, New York 10017.

Gramercy Books™ and design are trademarks of Random House Value Publishing, Inc.

Random House
New York • Toronto • London • Sydney • Auckland
http://www.randomhouse.com/

Cover and text Design: Karen Ocker

Printed and bound in Singapore

A CIP catalog record for this book is available from the Library of Congress.

ISBN 0-517-16308-X

8 7 6 5 4 3 2 1

CONTENTS

AFRICAN-AMERICAN HISTORY

According to the 1790 Census, the first, there were 697,897 enslaved blacks in the original thirteen states.

The first formal protest against slavery was signed by four Mennonite men in Germantown, Pennsylvania on February 18, 1688.

The first abolitionist group, the Pennsylvania Society for the Abolition of Slavery, was formed in Philadelphia by Quakers in 1775. Benjamin Franklin was its first president.

In 1777, Vermont, which was not even a state during the American Revolution, abolished slavery.

In 1780, Pennsylvania became the first state to abolish slavery.

Crispus Attucks, a black seaman and escaped slave from Framingham, Massachusetts, was the first man to die at the Boston Massacre in March of 1770. About 5,000 black patriots fought in the American Revolution against the British.

Paul Cuffe (1759-1817), a free black man, operated his own successful shipbuilding company in New England in the late 1700s and early 1800s. In 1780 Captain Cuffe and six other African-American residents of Massachusetts petitioned the state legislature for the right to vote. The courts agreed and they were awarded full civil rights.

The first African-American masonic lodge, African Lodge No. 459, was chartered in Boston, Massachusetts in 1787. It was founded by Prince Hall, a veteran of the Revolutionary War and landowner who had been denied membership in white masonic lodges.

The Bethel African Methodist Episcopal Church for Negroes was founded in 1794 in Philadelphia, Pennsylvania, by Richard Allen, a former slave. It sits on the oldest piece of real estate continuously owned by blacks in the United States. This was the first African Methodist Episcopal (A.M.E.) church in the world.

Chicago, Illinois was founded as a permanent settlement in 1773 by Jean Baptiste Point du Sable, an African-American merchant who was born in Haiti, the son of an African slave and a French seaman.

Blanche Kelso Bruce, a former slave who established a school for African-Americans in Hannibal, Missouri, in 1864, was the first African-American to serve a full six-year term in the U.S. Senate. His term ended in 1875.

Although Fisk University in Nashville, one of the earliest black universities in the United States, was founded by 1865, it did not have an African-American president until Charles Spurgeon Johnson was appointed in 1946.

Susie King Taylor (1842-1912) was an escaped slave who taught freed blacks to read and write. After meeting Clara Barton, she traveled with the 33rd U.S. Colored Troops as a nurse and launderer until the end of the Civil War.

During the Civil War, black soldiers in the Union Army had 220,000 African-Americans serving in the U.S.C.T., led by 7,000 white officers.

In 1862, slavery was abolished in Washington, D.C. Slave owners received compensation for their lost "property."

"Carry Me Back to Ol' Virginny," adopted as the official Virginia state song in 1940, was written by James A. Bland in 1878. Born to free parents in Flushing, New York in 1854, Bland attended Howard University and studied law before leaving school to join Callender's Original Georgia Minstrels.

In 1835, the Fifth National Negro Convention recommended that blacks remove the word "African" from the names of their organizations. It also asked blacks to stop referring to themselves as "colored."

On June 10, 1854, the first African-American Roman Catholic priest, James Augustine Healy, was ordained in Paris at Notre Dame Cathedral. In 1875, after consecration by Pope Pius IX, Healy became the first African-American bishop. His brother, Patrick Francis Healy, was the first African-American awarded a Ph.D. degree and the first African-American president of Georgetown University.

From 1860 until after World War II, the resort of Cape May, New Jersey was largely built and maintained by African-American labor and visited by African-Americans who lived there and many who summered there. In 1930, African-Americans represented 20% of the town's population.

Although the Quakers hold a reputation for fighting oppression and war, throughout the 19th century their meetings were segregated, with black members sitting in corners or underneath stairs and being guarded.

In April of 1907 Harlem Hospital in New York City, which would become on of the nation's leading African-American hospitals, opened with 150 beds for whites only.

Eatonville, Florida is the country's oldest surviving black municipality and the birthplace of Zora Neale Hurston, a prominent writer of the Harlem Renaissance.

American Beach, on Amelia Island off the northernmost Atlantic coast of Florida was established in the 1930s by A. L. Lewis, founder of the Afro-American Life Insurance Company, for his employees. The beach became popular with African-Americans denied access to most vacation sites in the South.

"Deadwood Dick," one of the best cowboys of his time was an African-American named Nat Love, born a Tennessee slave in 1854. After retirement he worked as a Pullman porter and a bank guard.

On November 30, 1830, the American Society of Free Persons of Colour met in Philadelphia, Pennsylvania, presided over by AME bishop Richard Allen. According to the U.S. Census Bureau, at the time of the convention there were 319,000 free men of color.

In 1866 the Freedman's Bureau opened 45 million acres of public lands in Alabama, Mississippi, Louisiana, Arkansas and

Florida. Many freedmen took advantage of the homestead opportunity, creating the first major wave of African-American land ownership. By 1890, there were 120,738 black farms and by 1910, there were 218,972 comprising nearly 15 million acres. During the twentieth century, African-Americans were consistently drawn to the industrialized North. In 1920 there were nearly 1 million African-American farmers in the U.S. Today there are fewer than 18,000, representing less than 1% of all farms.

The NAACP was founded as the National Negro Committee in 1909 on February 12th, Lincoln's birthday. W. E. B. DuBois was the only African-American officeholder of the NAACP in its early years.

In 1890 the black population of the United States was 8.3 million, 90% of it concentrated in the South.

Mary McLeod Bethune, the fifteenth of seventeen children born to former slaves in 1875, became a rights leader as well as an adviser to United States presidents and government officials, and is often considered one of the most influential African-American women in United States history. She founded the National Council of Negro Women in 1935, and a year later President Franklin D. Roosevelt appointed her Director of Negro Affairs for the National Youth Administration.

The first African-American women were sworn in as WAVES on December 13, 1944. This was the first women's branch of the U.S. armed forces to achieve full racial integration, although membership of black women remained small. During World War II, about 4,000 of the 350,000 women who served in the armed forces were African-American.

Although Elizabeth Ross Haynes served as the first black national secretary of the YWCA and in 1924 became the first black woman elected to the national board of the YWCA, a position she held until 1934, full integration of the YWCA did not happen until 1946.

In 1960 San Antonio, Texas became the first major Southern city to integrate lunch counters.

On October 25, 1976, Governor George Wallace of Alabama granted a full pardon to the last of the Scottsboro nine. Clarence Norris had been arrested in 1931, along with eight other African-Americans, convicted of rape and faced the death penalty. The Scottsboro Trial, the most notorious legal case forced the U. S. Supreme Court to acknowledge that the defendants had been denied due process and equal protection under the law.

Coretta Scott King, widow of the slain civil rights leader Martin Luther King, Jr., originally planned a vocal career. Born in Alabama, she won a scholarship to Antioch College in Ohio in 1945to study music and elementary education. While at Antioch, she performed in a program with famous African-American singer Paul Robeson. King received a scholarship to the New England Conservatory of Music in Boston in 1951. In 1953 she married Dr. King and returned with him to Alabama. King never found her career in music, but with her husband, became a major leader of the civil rights movement and continues to campaign for human rights, social justice, and urban renewal.

Before her arrest in 1955 for refusing to give up her bus seat to a white man in Montgomery, Alabama, Rosa Parks served as secretary of the Montgomery branch of NAACP and later advisor to the NAACP Youth Council. In 1999, Parks was awarded the Congressional Medal of Honor.

When Army General Colin Powell became Chairman of the Joint Chiefs of Staff in 1989, he became the military's highest-ranking African-American.

A United States Census Bureau report of 2000 projected that the African-American population is expected to grow more than twice as fast as the white population between 1995 and 2050.

FAMOUS FIRSTS

Booker T. Washington was the first African-American honored on a U.S. postage stamp when his image appeared on a new stamp in 1940.

Harriet Tubman became the first African-American woman honored on a postage stamp, but this didn't happen until 1978.

The first African-American honored with a National Holiday was Martin Luther King, Jr., whose birthday became a holiday on January 20, 1986, eighteen years after his assassination.

The first African-American formally admitted to the bar was Macon B. Allen. He passed the examinations in 1845, and practiced law in Massachusetts.

In 1872 Charlotte Ray received her law degree from Howard University Law School, making her the first black woman lawyer.

The first African-American to vote in the United States was Thomas Mundy Peterson. Peterson worked as a janitor in School 1, the first public school in Perth Amboy, New Jersey, built in 1871. The public school now carries his name and honors him each spring. Peterson voted as a result of the ratification in 1870 of the 15th Amendment, guaranteeing all Americans the right to vote.

A. Philip Randolph, born in Florida in 1889, and organized the International Brotherhood of Sleeping Car Porters, the first major all-black trade union. He was also the first African-American to serve as international vice-president of the AFL-CIO, formed in 1955.

Dr. Lucas Santomee, New York City's first black doctor, was the son of a slave who arrived in 1625 and was emancipated twenty years later.

The first black church wedding took place in 1641 at St. Nicholas church in New York between Anthony Van Angola and Lucie d'Angola.

The first legal adoption of a child by a black couple took place in 1661. Free citizen Emanuel Pietersen and Dorothy Angola petitioned the court for a "Certificate of Freedom" for Anthony Angola whom they adopted as a baby. They paid 300 guilders for him.

Benjamin O. Davis was the first African-American to reach the rank of general in the U.S. Army when President Franklin D. Roosevelt promoted him to brigadier general in 1940. He began his career with the Buffalo Soldiers in 1899, a private in one of the regiments created by Congress for black soldiers to serve in peacetime. Most of the Buffalo Soldiers' fought in Indian wars in the Dakotas, Texas, Colorado, Kansas, and Arizona, opening up new areas for American settlement.

Bessie Coleman, a native of Atlanta, Texas, learned French in order to study aviation in France. In 1921, she became the first African-American woman to earn an international pilot license.

On November 5, 1968, Shirley Chisholm became the first African-American woman to serve in the U.S. Congress. Born in New York to West Indian parents, she represented the Bedford-Stuyvesant section of Brooklyn.

It is an African-American doctor who is credited with performing the first successful open heart surgery. An 1883 graduate of Chicago Medical College, Daniel Hale Williams founded Provident

Hospital in 1891, the first interracial hospital in the United States. It was at Provident Hospital in Chicago that he performed the daring heart surgery in 1893. He opened the chest of a patient with a stab wound to the heart, sutured the wound, and closed the chest. The patient survived at least 20 years after the surgery.

Thurgood Marshall, who finished first in his class at Howard University Law School, became the first African-American Justice on the Supreme Court of the United States.

Reverend Hiram R. Revels served as a missionary in the South after the Civil War. In 1869, Revels was elected to the Mississippi State Senate and in 1870, he became the first black elected to the U.S. Senate, filling the seat vacated by Confederate President Jefferson Davis.

The first African-American man to win a Pulitzer Prize was Monete Sleet, Jr., a staff photographer for *Ebony* magazine. He was awarded the prize in 1969 for his photograph of Coretta Scott King and her daughter at the funeral of Dr. Martin Luther King, Jr. In 1970 Cheryl Adrienne Brown became the first African-American contestant for Miss America. Although from New York, Brown was in college in Iowa and represented that state.

 In 1950, Dr. Ralph Bunche was the first Black to receive the Nobel Peace Prize.

The first black man to graduate from an American College was John Russwurm from Bowdoin College in 1826. He was editor of the first black newspaper in the U.S. *Freedom's Journal*, a weekly published in New York from 1827-1829

In 1966, Dr. Robert Weaver was appointed by President Lyndon B. Johnson to head the newly created Department of Housing and Urban Development (HUD) and became the first African-American to serve in a presidential cabinet.

Rodeo star Bill Pickett was the first African-American elected to the Cowboy Hall of Fame in 1971. Called the Dusky Demon, he was one of the most popular cowboys of the 101 Ranch Wild West Show. He died in April 1932 after being kicked while roping a bronco.

Paul R. Williams, the first African-American member of the American Institute of Architects and known as the "architect to the stars" designed homes for Cary Grant, Frank Sinatra, Lucile Ball, Lon Chaney, Danny Thomas and others. He also designed the Los Angeles County and made alterations and additions to the Beverly Wilshire Hotel.

In 1989, the Reverend Barbara C. Harris was ordained as the first female bishop of the Episcopal Church. She was 58 years old and served the Episcopal Diocese of Massachusetts.

When he flew a Challenger mission in 1983, Guion Stewart Bluford, Jr. became the first African-American astronaut in space.

In August 1974, Beverly Johnson became the first African-American to appear on the cover of Vogue magazine.

Dr. Mae Jemison became the first African-American woman in space when she served about the space shuttle Endeavor in 1992.

Jane M. Bolin, the first African-American woman to graduate from Yale University Law School, was appointed America's first African-American woman judge in 1939. She was appointed to the Domestic Relations Court of the City of New York, which then became the Family Court of the State of New York and served until her retirement in 1978.

Explorer Matthew Alexander Henson became the first African-American to reach the North Pole in April 1909. Part of Admiral Robert E. Peary's expedition, Henson planted the American flag at 90 degrees north. The temperature was -29 degrees.

On January 2, 1990, David Dinkins became the first African-American mayor of New York City, America's largest city.

Yvonne Braithwaite Burke, a California Democrat, was the first African-American woman to represent California in the national government. She was also the first woman in the U.S. Congress to be granted maternity leave and in 1973 she became the first member of Congress to give birth while holding office.

Louis Tompkins Wright, born in 1891, was the first black surgeon to be appointed to all-white Harlem Hospital in New York. Four white doctors resigned in protest. He went on to become director of surgery and then president of the hospital's board. He became an authority on aureomycin, the first in the world to successfully experiment with this new antibiotic on humans.

In 1978, Joseph Freeman, 25, became the first known African-American to serve as a Mormon priest. This was of note because previously the Mormons preached that people were born into the black race as "punishment" for having failed God in a prior existence.

Barbara Jordan was the first African-American woman from the South to serve in the U.S. House of Representatives, from 1973-1979.

Reverend Jesse L. Jackson, one of America's foremost political figures in the past three decades--including positions as President of the National Rainbow Coalition and long-time assistant to

Dr. Martin Luther King, Jr. in the Southern Christian Leadership Conference--was the first African-American presidential candidate. His 1984 campaign won 3.5 million votes and registered over a million new voters; his 1988 candidacy won seven million votes and is said to have registered two million new voters.

Samuel L. Gravely, born in 1922, was the first African-American admiral in the U.S. Navy. He was also the first black person to command a United States warship.

Ronald H. Brown, who grew up in New York City in the 1940s and became lawyer, was elected chairman of the Democratic National Party in 1989, the first African-American to head a major political party. In 1993 he was appointed Secretary of Commerce and died in a plane crash in 1996 near the Croatian coast while on a mission.

In June of 1877, Henry O. Flipper, born a slave in Thomasville, Georgia, became the first African-American to graduate from West Point.

Body builder Chris Dickerson, became the first black Mr. America in 1970.

HOLIDAYS AND TRADITIONS

Jonkonnu (also known as Jonkankus or Johnkankus, in honor of an ancient African chief) is a pageant dating from the plantation era. Bands of colorful Jonkonnu troupes, dressed in costume with horse or cow heads, or as kings, queens, or devils, paraded through the streets in southeastern coast communities at Christmas time. They danced to the beat of drums and other instruments like the banjo, fife, and kitchen grater. The celebration died out among African-Americans in 1865 because of its association with slavery. Today it is still being celebrated in Jamaica.

Goober (peanut) comes from the Bantu word *nguba*.

Banjo comes from *mbanya*, a Kimbundu word meaning " stringed instrument."

September 10th is African-American Day in New York City.

Dr. Maulana Karenga, chair of the Department of Black Studies at California State University, Long Beach is known as the creator of Kwanzaa, an African-American holiday celebration. Kwanzaa is a Swahili word that means "first" and signifies the first fruits of the harvest. The American celebration takes place during the six days at the end of December.

Gele is the African head wrap representing Yoruba/Khemit culture.

The term "sell down the river" was first used in the 1830s and refers to a punishment that was a constant threat to slaves on the Upper Mississippi River. If they misbehaved, they were in danger of being sold to sugar plantation owners down the river, where the conditions were ever worse.

According to Early American Negroes in North Carolina, sneezing during a meal meant you would soon hear of a death.

According to early American Negro superstitions, May is an unlucky month in which to be married.

American Negro folklore say that if you cut a child's fingernails before the age of one, the child will become a thief.

Black Americans once used tea made from white ants to prevent or cure a case of whooping cough.

According to Southern Black folklore, wearing a buzzard feather behind your ear will prevent rheumatism, and buzzard feathers tied around a baby's neck will ease teething pain.

The West African custom of burying a baby's umbilical cord and celebrating with a feast afterward,was first brought to general attention as the "outdooring" custom on the eighth day of Kunte Kinte's life in Alex Haley's *Roots*. The Afrocentric Baby Shower, incorporating some of these traditions, has become a popular custom in the African-American community.

It was customary in the early years of Memorial Day, or Decoration Day—a holiday created after the Civil War to honor the war dead—for African-American church communities to spend the day cleaning and weeding the church cemetery, planting bushes or trees near the headstones, and paying tribute to family members with prayer. This was followed by a picnic-style dinner, called Memorial Day Dinner on the Grounds. This custom is being revived today in the African-American community.

Juneteenth, the holiday commemorating the day that the news of the Emancipation Proclamation reached Galveston, Texas— two and a half years after Lincoln signed it— is a popular African-American celebration all over the United States.

The Nine Night Ceremony is a West Indian practice similar to an Irish wake. The spirit of the dead is given nine nights of special attendance before being sent to the afterworld.

Many African-American parents have begun to embrace the ancient African tradition of the rites of passage ceremony as a way of recognizing their children's growth while grounding them in the traditions of African culture. After several months of study of African tradition, family history, community spirit, leadership skills, values, African art and dance, and more, the actually ceremony involves presentation to the community. The children dress in African-style clothing, receive a community blessing, are given gifts-jewelry for girls and an African walking stick or fly whisk (used by African royalty) for boys, and perform African song and dance. This is followed by a festive meal.

The Black Culinarian Alliance (BCA) was founded in 1993 by Jason Wallace and Alex Askew as an alumni chapter of the Culinary Institute of America. It is the leading African-American culinary association in the U.S. and its membership includes culinary experts and food service professionals from across the country. In addition to representing minorities in the food industry, BCA highlights African-American food traditions originating in both Africa and the Caribbean, and African-American inventors in the culinary world.

SCIENCE AND EDUCATION

One year after the first shipload of captive Africans landed at Jamestown, Virginia in 1619, a school was established to educate both blacks and Indians in Virginia.

The first school for African-American children in New York City was the African Free School, founded by the New York Manumission Society, an abolitionist society, in 1787. It began with an enrollment of 40 students.

In 1834, South Carolina passed a law making it a crime for African-Americans, free or slaves, to be educated.

Howard University, the third university in Washington, D.C., was founded in 1866 by ten members of the First Congregational

Society of Washington seeking to create a seminary for the training of black ministers. Its original name was Howard Normal and Theological Institute for the Education of Teachers and Preachers, named for Civil War hero General Oliver O. Howard who was Commissioner of the Freedman's Bureau. In January of 1867 its name was changed to Howard University and on March 2, 1867 it was officially incorporated by congressional charter. Most of the financial support for the university came from the Freedmen's Bureau. In 1879, Congress approved a special appropriation.

Booker T. Washington, president of Tuskegee Institute and author of Up From Slavery, became the first African-American to be awarded an honorary degree at Harvard in 1896.

Oberlin College, founded in Oberlin, Ohio, in 1833, in 1834 became the first institution of higher learning in America to admit both women and African-Americans.

Mary Church Terrell, an 1884 graduate of Oberlin College, was the first African-American woman appointed to the school board of Washington D.C. in 1895. She was also a founder of the National Association of Colored Women and served as its president. First public school system for blacks was opened in DC in 1864.

Carter G. Woodson, the founder of Negro History Week in 1926, was a brilliant student who was unable to attend high school until he was twenty because he was forced to work in the coal mines in Virginia. In 1976 Negro History Week became Black History Month.

Alain Locke, the son of a Philadelphia schoolteacher, graduated from Harvard University and in 1907 the first African-American awarded a Rhodes scholarship to study at Oxford University in England. He was an internationally known figure in education and in 1945 was elected the first African-American president of the American Association for Adult Education, a predominantly white organization.

The first African-American of the "Little Rock Nine" to graduate from Little Rock High School was Ernest Green. After receiving degrees from Michigan State University, Green served as assistant secretary of labor for employment and training under President Carter, formed a consulting firm specializing in employment and training services for minorities, and became a senior vice president of the Lehman Brothers investment banking firm. He also has served on the board of directors of the NAACP, the Winthrop Rockefeller Foundation, the Eisenhower World Affairs Institute, and the Quality Education for Minorities Network.

The first college devoted to the education of African-Americans was established in Pennsylvania in 1854. It was named Ashmun Institute, after the first president of Liberia, but in 1866 its name was changed to Lincoln University in memory of Abraham Lincoln.

Cheney University in Pennsylvania was actually started in 1837 as a high school for African-Americans. It was called the Institute for Colored Youth and was started with money left by a Quaker. Cheney did not actually become a fully accredited college until 1951.

In 1987, Spelman College, the oldest and largest black college for women in the United States, had its first black woman president since its founding in 1800.

When people ask for the "real McCoy" they want to be sure that they get the real item and not a cheap substitute. The expression is named for Elijah McCoy (1844-1929), an African-American inventor born to fugitive slave parents in Ontario, Canada. McCoy held more than 500 patents, but his first famous invention was for a self-lubricating device for industrial machinery. It constantly fed oil into heavy machinery so that it did not have to be shut down for oiling, a process that wasted a great deal of time, money, and energy.

George Washington Carver, the man who found more than 350 uses for peanuts, sweet potatoes and pecans, actually received his undergraduate degree in art. Carver, known as the "Wizard of Tuskegee," was born a slave in Missouri in 1864, worked as a field hand after the Civil War to obtain a high school education and was the first black student admitted to Simpson College. Some of his paintings were displayed at the Columbian Exposition in Chicago in 1893. Carver received a degree in agriculture in 1894 from Iowa Agricultural College and was hired by Booker T. Washington to teach and do research at Tuskegee Institute in Alabama.

By 1913, an estimated 800 to 1,200 patents were issued to blacks for their inventions.

In 1892 Sarah Boone patented an ironing board with "edges curved to correspond to the outside and inside seams of a sleeve."

Henry Blair was the first African American to receive a U.S. Patent on October 14, 1834, for his corn harvester.

Percy Julian, who secured 86 patents, was born in 1898 in Montgomery, Alabama, the son of a railroad clerk. Among his best known discoveries are a synthetic drug used for the treatment of glaucoma and a method of producing sterols that greatly reduced their cost and ultimately could be derived into cortisone.

According to the United States Census of 1998, in 1996, 74%
of the nation's African-Americans aged 25 and over had at least
a high school diploma, up from 51% in 1980.

According to the United States Census of 1998, about 40% of
African-American three- and four-year-olds were enrolled in
nursery school in 1995, the same proportion as white Americans.

The clothes dryer was invented by G. T. Sampson in 1892.

L. J. Love received a patent on his
pencil sharpener in November of 1897.

In 1883, Jan Ernst Matzeliger, patented his shoe-lasting
machine, which increased worker productivity from 60 pairs
of shoes per day to more than 400. It remains the basic device
used by the modern shoe industry.

W. D. Davis invented the horse saddle.

According to the American Association of Engineering Societies,
African-Americans received 4% of the total engineering degrees
in the United States in 1998.

Louis Howard Latimer, a draftsman, inventor, and a member
of the Edison Pioneers (a group of scientists who worked with

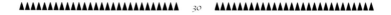

Thomas Edison), was given a patent in 1882 for the process of manufacturing carbon filaments used in electric lamps. He had earlier patented an electric lamp commonly known as the Latimer lamp and had also prepared the drawings for Alexander Graham Bell's 1876 telephone.

In 1754, when he was only twenty-four years old, a freeborn Negro from Maryland, Benjamin Banneker, built what is believed to be the first clock made in the United States.

In 1848, Lewis Temple invented a toggle-harpoon that revolutionized the whaling industry and became the standard.

Norbert Rillieux, born in New Orleans in 1806—the son of the master of a plantation and one of his slaves. His father sent him to Paris where as a black man he could receive a good education. In 1843, Rillieux, chief engineer in a New Orleans sugar refinery, invented a vacuum evaporation system to refining sugar that both improved the quality and cut production costs, making sugar more affordable. He became one of the wealthiest and important men in Louisiana. Eleven years later, when in New Orleans, Rillieux faced such severe restrictions—in 1854 in spite of his wealth he was required to carry a pass to travel freely around the city—Rillieux left the United States for France.

Granville T. Woods, born in 1856 in Columbus, Ohio, who left school at the age of ten and worked as a mechanic is often called the "Black Edison." He was able to return to school in 1876 to study mechanical engineering. He is credited with more than 50 patented inventions, including the Synchronous Multiplex Railway Telegraph, a telephone, which he sold to the Bell Telephone Company, the automatic air brake (which he sold to George Westinghouse), a steam boiler furnace, and an incubator.

 In July 1885 a patent was awarded to Sarah E. Goode, the owner of a Chicago furniture manufacturer, for a "Folding Cabinet Bed."

Ronald E. McNair, African-American physicist and astronaut, was one of the victims of the space shuttle Challenger explosion in 1986.

African-American Charles R. Drew, born in 1904, created the plasma method of blood preservation and received the NAACP's Spingarn Medal in 1944 for his contributions to science.

In 1970, Dr. Hugh S. Scott of Washington, D.C. became the first African-American superintendent of schools in a major U.S. city.

LITERATURE AND THE ARTS

Sculptor Meta Fuller, born in Philadelphia, Pennsylvania in 1877, studied in Paris with Auguste Rodin. Her works were exhibited in Paris as well as all over the United States.

The first successful black cartoonist was E.Simms Campbell, who drew "Cuties" in the 1940s and was creator of the mustachioed roue character Esky. Campbell's work appeared in every issue of Esquire magazine from 1933 to 1971.

The Associated Negro Press (ANP), the first national news service for African-American newspapers was established in 1919.

In February of 1956, L. R. Lautier was the first African-American admitted to the all-male, all-white National Press Club.

In 1937, William Edmondson, born in Nashville, Tennessee in about 1882, was the first African-American artist—famous for his tombstone carvings—to have a solo exhibit at the Museum of

Modern Art in New York City. He never received formal training as an artist.

In 1944, Dr. Frederick Douglass Patterson, president of Tuskeegee Institute founded the United Negro College Fund (UNCF).

In 1968, Elizabeth Duncan Koontz, a special education teacher in North Carolina, was elected president of the National Education Association, the first African-American in that position.

Frances Ellen Watkins Harper was the most famous African-American poet of the nineteenth century. She wrote more than a dozen books, and in 1896 she helped establish the National Association of Colored Women.

Alexander Pushkin, one of the greatest poets in Russian history and known as the "father" of Russian literature, was the great-grandson of an African slave who moved up from slavery to become a general under Peter the Great.

The first novel by an African-American woman was *Our Nig: Sketches from the Life of a Free Black,* written by Harriet Wilson and published in 1859.

Phyllis Wheatley, born in 1753 in Senegal West Africa and sold from a slave ship into a Boston, Massachusetts family, is considered the first African-American woman of poet of note in the United States. Her first volume of poetry was published in 1773.

In 1998 Chicago State University established the Literary Hall of Fame for Writers of African Descent. The first inductee was John A. Williams, the author who won the American Book Award for his 1982 novel *!Click Song*. There are now 69 inductees including Ishmael Reed.

Ralph Ellison's *Invisible Man*, the saga of a black man's struggle for identity in white America, won the National Book Award in 1953. Ellison attended Alabama's Tuskeegee Institute in the 1930s. His final novel, Juneteenth, was published posthumously in 1999.

Alice Walker won the Pulitzer Prize in 1983 for her novel *The Color Purple*. The novel also won the American Book Award for fiction in the same year.

Zora Neale Hurston, the most prominent African-American woman writer of the Harlem Renaissance, died on welfare in Fort Pierce, Florida. Her grave was unmarked until Alice Walker, who brought Hurston's writing back into popularity, arranged for a headstone. The Zora Neal Hurston Festival of the Arts and Humanities is held each year in the all-black town of Eatonville, Florida, where Hurston was born.

Gordon Parks, Jr. was the first African-American staff photographer for *Life* magazine and was also the first black person to direct movies for a major studio. He received an Emmy award in 1968 for his documentary film *Diary of a Harlem Family*.

James M. Rodger, Jr. of Durham, North Carolina became the first African-American to be named National Teacher of the Year in 1972.

Playwright August Wilson was a two-time Pulitzer Prize winner and in 1987 he won a Tony Award for his play, *Fences*.

Paul Laurence Dunbar, born in Dayton, Ohio in June 1872 was a prolific and popular turn-of-the-twentieth-century writer. His first volume of poetry, *Oak and Ivory*, was published in 1892 with the help of friends Orville and Wilbur Wright.

John James Audubon, known as the painter of Birds of America, was 1/2 African-American. His mother was African-Caribbean.

Archibald J. Motley, an artist born in New Orleans, Louisiana in 1891, was one of the first African-American artists to have a one-man show at a New York gallery. Motley was raised in Chicago and studied at the Art Institute. His themes included African scenes and voodoo dances.

Gloria Naylor's first novel, *The Women of Brewster Place*, won the American Book Award for fiction in 1983. The novel was made into a television movie starring Oprah Winfrey.

Native Son, written by Richard Wright and published in 1940, was the first book by a black person to become a Book-of-the-Month Club selection.

In 1993, Rita Dove was named America's Poet Laureate, the first African-American and the youngest poet to hold that post. In 1987 she received a Pulitzer Prize for her third book of poetry, *Thomas and Beulah*.

Ernest Gaines, author of the critically acclaimed *Autobiography of Miss Jane Pittman*, won the National Book Critics Circle Award for *A Lesson Before Dying*, which was selected for the Oprah Winfrey Book Club in 1997.

In 1993, Toni Morrison became the first African-American woman to win a Nobel Prize for literature. Her novel, *Beloved*, won the Pulitzer Prize for fiction in 1988 and *Song of Solomon*, published in 1977, won the National Book Critics Award and was a main selection of the Book-of-the-Month Club, only the second book by an African-American to be chosen since Richard Wright's *Native Son* in 1941.

Chicago-born poet Gwendolyn Brooks was the African-American to win the Pulitzer Prize. She received it in 1950 for her second collection of poetry, *Annie Allen*. She was designated poet laureate of Illinois in 1968 and in 1985 she became the first African-American woman to be appointed poetry consultant at the Library of Congress.

In 1942 the first volume of poetry by Margaret Walker, *For My People*, was chosen for the Yale Young Poet Series. She was only 27 years old. She is best known for her later novel, *Jubilee*, a standard in many literature curricula.

Romare Bearden, born in Charlotte, North Carolina in 1914 is known as one of the finest artists of the twentieth century. He was elected to the American Academy of Arts and Letters, the National Institute of Arts and Letters, and received the President's National Medal of Arts in 1987.

Writer Maya Angelou was the first black woman to speak at a presidential inauguration. As a teenager she worked as San Francisco's first female streetcar conductor. Active in the Civil Rights Movement, Angelou lived in Africa working as a journalist and university professor and then returned to the U.S. and became of part of the Harlem Writers Guild. Her autobiography, *I Know Why the Caged Bird Sings*, was published in 1970 and became a bestseller. Angelou's first published book of poetry, *Just Give Me a Cool Drink of Water,* was published in 1971 and nominated for a Pulitzer Prize. The poem she read at President Bill Clinton's 1993 inauguration was "On the Pulse of the Morning."

Henry Ossawa Tanner was the first African-American artist elected to the National Academy of Design. In 1973 the U.S. Postal Service issued a stamp commemorating his work.

Richard Hunt, born in Chicago in 1935, graduated from the Art Institute of Chicago, studied in Europe, and became one of the leading sculptors in the United States. His sculpture is shown in the National Museum of American Art, the Whitney Museum of American Art, and the Metropolitan Museum of Art.

The Schomburg Center for Research in Black Culture is one of the most widely used research facilities in the world devoted to the preservation of materials on African-American life. A branch of the New York Public Library, the collection is a major institution of the Harlem Community, named in honor of distinguished Black scholar and bibliophile, Arthur A. Schomburg, was added. It included over 5,000 volumes, 3,000 manuscripts, 2,000 etchings and paintings and several thousand pamphlets. Schomburg served as its curator from 1932 until his death in 1938.

BUSINESS

Booker T. Washington founded the National Negro Business League in 1900. By 1915, it had 600 state and local branches.

According to the U.S. Census Bureau, the number of African-American-owned businesses in the United States increased 46% between 1978 and 1992.

John H. Johnson, born in Arkansas City, Arkansas in 1918 and founder and publisher of *Ebony* magazine, is ranked among America's 400 richest people. Johnson's first magazine, *Negro Digest*, modeled after Reader's Digest, was founded in 1942 and *Ebony* followed in 1945, with an initial sale of 25,000 copies. In addition to publishing magazines and books, Johnson founded Fashion Fair Cosmetics, the Supreme Life Insurance Company, and television and radio stations.

The St. Luke Penny Savings Bank was opened in 1903 in Richmond, Virginia by Maggie Lena Walker. Now known as Consolidated Bank and Trust Company, it is America's oldest continually operated minority-owned bank and the tenth largest African-American owned bank in the U.S. Walker was born to a poor family in Richmond, Virginia. In 1889, after completing a course in business training, she became executive secretary of the Independent Order of St. Luke Society, an African-American organization for the sick and elderly that also provided burial services. She expanded the society into an insurance company and in 1903 she added the bank. She was the first woman in America to be a bank president.

Created in 1987, the Mahogany line of Hallmark Cards, Inc. has more than 800 greeting cards, the largest brand of cards for African-Americans.

According to the 1992 U.S. Census, the city with the highest concentration of African-American business firms was Washington, D.C., with African-American firms representing 29% of the business firms.

The 1992 U.S. Census notes that the number of African-American-owned businesses increased 46% between 1987 and 1992; the national increase for the same period was 26%.

The inventor of Famous Amos chocolate chip cookies was Wally Amos, an African-American Hollywood Press agent, who used his Aunt Della's recipe. A great self-promoter, he opened a cookie stand on Sunset Boulevard and even printed t-shirts, posters, and bumpers with his logo.

The original Aunt Jemima® was Nancy Green, a famous African-American cook hired by the Davis Milling Company to promote of packaged pancake mix at the 1893 Columbian Exposition in Chicago. She was a success and by the time the fair was over, more than a million pancakes had been served. She continued to pose as Aunt Jemima at fairs and expositions all across the national until her death in 1923 at the age of 89.

In 1897, a black American waiter in Chicago was discovered by the manufacturer of Cream of Wheat®, who asked him to pose in a chef's uniform for possible use as a trademark. The waiter was paid $5, but when the photo was approved for use as a trademark, the waiter could not be found. Although his portrait is now nationally recognized, he never received any further payment because no one could locate him.

The Afro-American Insurance Company, established in Philadelphia in 1810, the first known to be owned and managed by African-Americans, was founded to provide African-Americans with a proper burial.

The National Black MBA Association, an organization of more than 2,000 holders of advanced business degrees, was incorporated in 1972 to help minorities in the business community. William A. Liedesdorff, who arrived in California from the Virgin Islands in 1841, was influential in the development of San Francisco. Already a wealthy man, Liedesdorff bought land, built a home, and opened a store. He served as a member of the city council, was instrumental in setting up the first public school, launched the first steamboat on San Francisco Bay, and later opened the city's first hotel.

The first national African-American labor union in the United States, the Colored National Labor Union, was founded by Isaac Myers, a man who had established a black-owned cooperative shipyard to help African-American shipyard workers and long-shoremen pushed out of work at the end of the Civil War. He became its first president.

According to a report in *The Black Business Journal*, in 1996 Texaco paid the largest employment discrimination settlement to date by agreeing to pay $175 million to African-American employees. Several large employment discrimination cases by minorities against major corporations are still pending.

The first line of African-American beauty products in America was developed by Madame C. J. Walker, born Sarah Breedlove in Delta, Louisiana in 1867. Walker began by creating a formula to groom and condition African-American hair and eventually built her business by adding toiletries and cosmetics that were very popular among African-Americans, as well as opening beauty culture schools throughout the United States and the Caribbean. She is known as the first African-American woman millionaire.

The first African-American owned and operated record company, the Pace Phonograph Corporation, was established by Harry Pace in 1921. Pace had originally partnered with the famous blues composer W. C. Handy to found a music publishing company, but their partnership dissolved when Pace switched to records. His Black Swan label had its first hit with a recording of "Down Home Blues" and "Oh, Daddy," by Ethel Waters. In spite of some outstanding records, Pace was forced to declare bankruptcy in 1923 and sold the Black Swan label to Paramount Records.

African-Americans had no seats on the New York Stock Exchange until 1970, when Joseph L. Searles III, an aide to New York City Mayor John Lindsay, became a floor trader and general partner for Newburger, Loeb and Company. Two years later, Jerome Holland, former ambassador to Sweden and American college president became the first African-American on the board of directors of the New York Stock Exchange.

Black Enterprise Magazine was founded in 1970 as a magazine for black business owners and executives. According to a recent subscriber study, *Black Enterprise* readers are prominent, well educated and well employed, with an average income of over $73,500, and 23% either own their own businesses or are partners.

In 1971, the first African-American-owned company was listed on the American Stock Exchange. The Johnson Products Company, based in Chicago, specializing in cosmetic products for African-Americans, was founded in 1954 by George and John Johnson on $250 they borrowed. In 1993, the company was bought by IVAX, a Miami-based pharmaceutical company for $67 million.

Henry G. Parks, Jr., a marketing graduate of Ohio State University founded the Parks Sausage Company in Baltimore in 1951. The company struggled in its first years, but expanded rapidly, adding new products and sales areas.

In 1989, Maria Dowd left her job with a southern California promotions company to start her own company PROMO Trends, offering marketing and public relations services to local black-owned businesses. In 1991, she launched African-American Women on Tour, the first independent, nationally touring career empowerment conferences series for African-American women. She started PROMO trends with $1,000 borrowed from her parents.

The first African-American to make the *Forbes Magazine* list of the nation's 400 wealthiest people was Reginald Lewis. As a child in Baltimore, Lewis sold newspapers. He became a successful lawyer, and by 1992, owned TLC Beatrice International, the country's largest black-owned business and was listed by *Forbes* as having $400 million in personal assets. He died a year later of brain cancer at the age of 50. He was a generous donor and his $3 million dollar donation to his alma mater, Harvard Law School, in 1992 was their largest individual donation in its history. Harvard named its international law center in his honor, the first building at Harvard to be named for an African-American.

In 1998, Axis Fin, Ltd., a California-based financial service firm, partnered with Key Bank & Trust of Maryland to launch the AFRIcard MasterCard. The card's design uses African-American colors and carries the line, "the Soul of Money."

According to a 1997 study of wages and salaries conducted by Chicago-based Target Market News, African-American buying power increased to $392 billion, up 7% from the preceding year. Much of the credit goes to highly-educated black women, whose numbers in the work force and increased spending has risen steadily.

Delano E. Lewis, the first African-American president of National Public Radio, was previously president and CEO of the Chesapeake & Potomac Telephone Company, serving the Washington, D.C. area and one of the first telephone companies in the county to become involved in cable television. His earlier career included a period as attorney for the U.S. Department of Justice, as Peace Corps director in Africa, and jobs on Capitol Hill.

The first African-American Barbie was "Christie," created in 1968 by Mattel.

In 1999, the U.S. Agriculture Department settled a class action suit of about $1 billion brought by black farmers who accused the agency of discrimination in lending practices.

SPORTS

African-American Jack Johnson defeated James J. Jeffries, the "great white hope," in a boxing match in Reno, Nevada in 1910.

The golf tee was patented by African-American George F. Grant in 1899. Grant was a Harvard-educated dentist.

"Rube" Foster, born in Calvert, Texas, in 1879 founded the first African-American professional baseball league in 1920. Foster was inducted into the Baseball Hall of Fame in 1981 by the Veterans Committee.

Frederick Douglas "Fritz" Pollard, who played running back for the Brown University football team, was the first African-American to play in the Rose Bowl, when Brown played Washington State on New Year's Day 1916.

Moses Fleetwood Walker was the first African-American Major League Baseball player, 60 years before the Brooklyn Dodgers signed Jackie Robinson. Walker, a graduate of Oberlin College played in 42 games for the Toledo Baseball Club of the American Association in 1884. The American Association was considered a baseball major league until 1891.

Larry Doby, with 253 career home runs, was the first African-American player in the American league. He made his debut with the Cleveland Indians in 1947, only three months after.

Jackie Robinson appeared for the Brooklyn Dodgers. He led the Indian to two pennants and one World Championship and appeared in six all-star games.His fame was sometimes eclipsed by Jackie Robinson, but in 1998 he was elected to the Baseball Hall of Fame by the Veterans Committee.

Frank Robinson was the first black manager in major league baseball.

Alice Coachman was the first black woman to win Olympic Gold when she won the medal for the high jump in the 1948 London Olympics.

Arthur Ashe was the first black man to win a grand slam tennis tournament when he won the men's singles titles at the U.S. Open in 1968.

Jesse Owens, who won 4 gold medals in track and field at the 1936 Olympic games in Berlin—in spite of Adolf Hitler's claim that

black athletes were inferior—broke 5 world records and tied a 6th, all within 45 minutes during his sophomore year at Ohio State.

Legendary pitcher and Baseball Hall of Famer Bob Gibson suffered from rickets and asthma as a child and also had a heart murmur.

On February 8, 1986, 18-year-old Debi Thomas became the first African-American to win the women's Senior Singles U. S. Figure Skating Championship and the first African-American woman to win the women's World Figure Skating Championship.

Sugar Ray Robinson was the only boxer in history to become world middleweight champion five times. He was inducted into the International Boxing Hall of Fame in 1990.

Shaquille O'Neal was named Player of the Year by *Sports Illustrated* after his sophomore year of college at LSU.

In 1961, Ernie Davis, a member of the Syracuse University football team, became the first African-American to win the

Heisman Memorial Trophy. After college he was signed by the Cleveland Brown, but never played for them because he died of leukemia at the age of 23.

Horse racing in the 1800s was dominated by African-American jockeys. They won 15 of the first 28 Kentucky Derbys. The first African-American jockey to win the Kentucky Derby 3 times was Isaac Burns Murphy, known as the great jockey of the nineteenth century with 628 wins out of 1,412 races.

Charles Follis, who signed with the Shelby Blues in Shelby, Ohio in 1904, was the first African-American professional football player. He was badly injured in a 1906 Thanksgiving Day game and retired from football.

America's first candy bar named for a black athlete was the Reggie, manufactured by Standard Brands, in honor of baseball great Reggie Jackson.

"The Fastest Bicycle Rider in the World" was an African-American named Marshall Taylor. Born in Indiana in 1878, he first entered the sport as a trick rider for a bicycle shop. He was a member of an African-American cycling group called the See Saw Club. In 1898 Taylor became the cycling champion of America, the first African-American to capture a championship in any sport. Boxer Sam Lanford, known as the "Boston Terror," was actually born in Weymouth Falls, Nova Scotia in 1886.

▼▼▼

Hank Aaron is the all-time greatest home-run hitter in the major leagues. Because his high school didn't have a baseball team, Aaron's first experience with organized baseball was playing on a sandlot team called the Pritchett Athletics. By junior year of high school, he was playing part-time with the Mobile Black Bears, and at the age of 17, in 1951, he signed his first professional contract for $200 a month with the Indianapolis Clowns, a Negro League team with a strong following in the African-American community. At this point Aaron still had to be taught to bat correctly. A quick learner, in his first season he went on to lead the Negro League with a batting average of .467.

Tiger Woods, whose father is African-American and whose mother is Thai, was the first African-American to win a major golf tournament. Woods began playing golf when he began walking, and by the age of three was able to shoot a 48 for nine holes.

Lee Elder was the first African-American professional golfer to earn over $1 million.

In April 1966, Emmet Ashford became the first African-American major league umpire.

Florence Griffith-Joyner holds the world records as the fastest woman ever.

Black American boxing champion Joe Louis
lost just once in a 15-year span from 1934 to 1949.

Michael Jordan, a member of the 1992 and 1996
gold-medal U.S. Olympic basketball team, is the only professional
basketball player to receive the league's MVP four times.

George Branham, a twenty-four-year-old Californian, became
the first African-American to win a Professional Bowlers
Association event, the Brunswick Memorial World Open in 1987.

Leroy "Satchel" Paige became the first African-American pitcher
in the major leagues when he was signed by the Cleveland
Indians in 1948. He posted a 6-1 record for the World Champion
Indians in his first year.

In 1929 Reginald Weird, captain of the tennis team at City College
in New York was barred from the National Junior Indoor Tennis
Tournament of the U.S. Lawn Tennis Association. It was not until
1948 that Weird was allowed to participate in a tournament.

On March 2, 1962, Philadelphia 76er Wilt Chamberlain scored 100
points in a game against the New York Knicks. No other NBA
player (other than Chamberlain himself) has equaled this record.
The first game of the National Negro Baseball League (NNL)
was played in Indianapolis, Indiana in April of 1920.

▼▼

Muhammad Ali's 1976 match with Leon Spinks boasted the
biggest attendance in boxing history.

Jersey Joe Walcott, a black American was the oldest prizefighter
to hold the world's Heavyweight Championship title. Born in
Merchantville, New Jersey, Arnold Raymond.

Bill Russell became the first black coach of a major
pro-basketball team when he joined the Boston Celtics
in 1966. In 1967 the Celtics won the NBA championship.

Marion Jones, born in Los Angeles, California, in 1975 is one of the
United States' most impressive sprinters and Olympic hopefuls.
She began winning state 100- and 200-meter races at the age of 15
and went on to win many ACC championships. In 1992 she was
selected "High School Athlete of the Year" and in 1998 was named
Track & Field News' Athlete of the Year. In the last several years
she has taken home many USA Championships, wins at Goodwill
Games and World Cup championships in races as well as long
jumps. Jones was also a talented basketball player in high school
 and college but chose track as her sport through the
inspiration of Florence Griffith-Joyner. Jones is married
to world-class shot putter C. J. Hunter.

MUSIC AND ENTERTAINMENT

Born in New York in 1927 to West Indian parents, Harry Belafonte spent part of his childhood in Jamaica and earned fame as a singer of "calypso" music. Belfafonte received an Emmy awarded in 1960 for his television special, "Tonight with Belafonte." He received the 1999 NAACP Image Award and was named cultural advisor to the Peace Corps by John F. Kennedy. Actor and singer Paul Robeson was the first African-American to play Othello on an American stage with a white cast. He received the NAACP's Springarn award in 1945. He made his film debut in Oscar Micheaux's movie *Body and Soul* in 1925.

"Lift Ev'ry Voice and Sing," considered by most to be the black national anthem, was written in 1900 by James Weldon Johnson (who became general secretary of the NAACP in 1920) and his brother John Rosamond Johnson.

One of Mattel's earliest black "Barbies" was Julia, modeled after Diahann Carroll, the first African-American woman to be featured in her own television series, *Julia*. One of the two original versions produced in 1969 was "Talking Julia," who was dressed in a silver and gold jumpsuit and used Diahann Carroll's voice.

Soul music star, Jackie Wilson, known for his top songs including "Lonely Teardrops" and "I'll Be Satisfied," won boxing's Golden Glove competition at the age of 16 but was encouraged by his mother to go into music.

"Fats" Waller's most famous song, "Ain't Misbehavin" was recorded in 1929 in Camden, New Jersey, and was introduced in the Broadway hit *Hot Chocolates*.

The Fisk Jubilee Singers were formed in the 1860s to raise funds for the failing Fisk University. In 1871 they made their first national tour, their popular concerts, which introduced traditional black spirituals to audiences around the world. They performed at the White House for President Chester A. Arthur in 1882.

Radio personality Tom Joyner, called the "Fly Jock," received the President's Award at the NAACP's Image Awards, has been a four-time *Billboard Magazine* award winner and was the first African-American to be inducted into the Radio Hall of Fame.

In 1963 Sidney Poitier became the first African-American male to receive the Academy Award for his performance in *Lilies of the Field*.

The first black daily newspaper in America (1864), the New Orleans *Tribune*, was bilingual in French and English.

Oprah Winfrey got her first breakthrough in 1976 when she became co-anchor and reporter for WJZ-TV in Baltimore, the first African-American woman in the country to hold such a position. *The Oprah Winfrey Show*, broadcast from Chicago, is the highest-ranked talk show in television history with 15 to 20 million viewers daily and has received 25 Emmy Awards.

The first New York theater for blacks only was established in 1821. The African Grove Theater at Bleecker and Mercer Streets catered to audiences of free blacks. The first great American black actor, Ira Aldridge, made his stage debut here when still an adolescent. He achieved fame for his Victorian roles.

Famous performer Josephine Baker, considered one of the most colorful performers of all time, won the French Legion Medal of Honor for her services in the French resistance in occupied France during World War II.

In 1968, the K.C. Troupe was the first African-American act ever to appear in Ringling Bros. and Barnum & Bailey Circus.

They were discovered by producer and circus owner Irvin Feld when they auditioned for him on the sidewalk outside Madison Square Garden.

The first black-owned radio station, WEDR, began broadcasting in Atlanta, Georgia in 1949.

In 1973, WGPR-TV (Channel 62) in Detroit became the first television station owned by African-Americans.

Quincy Jones, African-American arranger, composer, and entertainment industry icon holds the all-time record for Grammy nominations with 77; he has received 26 Grammy awards and the Grammy Living Legend Award. In 1985 Jones produced the best-selling single of all time, "We Are the World."

Lorraine Hansberry became the first African-American woman to win the New York Drama Critics Circle Award for her play, *A Raisin in the Sun.* It opened in 1959 with Claudia McNeil and Sidney Poitier in the lead roles.

Michael Jackson's 1979 solo album *Off the Wall,* sold 7 million copies worldwide, surpassed only by *Thriller,* his largest-selling album with over 30 million copies sold, which included 7 top-ten hits and won the Grammy Award for best album of 1983.
The first African-American actor to star in a TV series was Bill Cosby in *I Spy,* which went on the air in 1965. It

won Cosby three consecutive Emmy awards. The weekly series about the Huxtable family, *The Cosby Show,* where he portrayed a doctor whose wife is a lawyer, was at one time the most popular situation comedy on television.

Berry Gordy started Motown, his entertainment empire incorporated in April 1960, in his home with a total investment of $800 he borrowed from his family. Gordy, a former factory worker originally chose the name Hitsville, USA, and then changed it by abbreviating the African-American slang name for Detroit, Motor Town. Motown moved from Detroit to Los Angeles in 1969.

Gail Fisher, who co-starred in the television detective show *Mannix* as Mannix's Girl Friday, was the first African-American woman to win an Emmy for her supporting role.

Hattie McDaniel became the first African-American to receive an Academy Award. She won as best supporting actress in the 1939 film *Gone with the Wind.*

In 1950, Juanita Hall became the first African-American to win a Tony award for her role as Bloody Mary in the musical *South Pacific.*

Marian Anderson, a star of the Metropolitan Opera in New York City and a recipient of the Presidential Medal of Freedom, was banned in 1939 from performing at Washington, D.C.'s Constitutional Hall, owned by the Daughters of the American Revolution. The concert was rescheduled as an outdoor free concert at the Lincoln Memorial, arranged by Eleanor Roosevelt, who resigned from the DAR.

Mahalia Jackson, the famous gospel singer, recorded two songs in 1937 that marked the introduction of the organ into Gospel music. Her break came in 1946 when she signed with Apollo Records, and her recording of "Move On Up a Little Higher" sold more than a million copies. In 1954 she was hired by CBS to star in a weekly Gospel television show.

William "Count" Basie, who won three Grammy Awards and Kennedy Center Honors, was born in 1904 in Red Bank, New Jersey. The Count Basic Orchestra opened at the Apollo Theatre in Harlem in 1937 with Billie Holiday as the vocalist.

The Cotton Club, located on the second floor of 644 Lexington at the corner of West 142nd Street in Harlem in New York City, was owned by a consortium of mobsters led by bootlegger Owney Madden. While the club featured black entertainers and waiters, its audience was white only. In 1927, Duke Ellington's band appeared at the Cotton Club for the first time. The weekly broadcasts on radio station WHN were heard all over the country and made Ellington and his Cotton Club Orchestra famous. Lena Horne got her start at the Cotton Club.

The famous "Negro" song "Ol' Man River" was written by the songwriting team of Oscar Hammerstein and Jerome Kern.

The Guinness Book of World Records recognizes Diana Ross as the most successful female artist in history. The Supremes were originally known as The Primettes, formed by the teenage Ross and friends Mary Wilson, Florence Ballard and Betty Anderson (later replaced by Barbara Martin) and sang back up for the Primes (later known as the Temptations).

Jelly Roll Morton, innovative piano soloist, composer, and arranger claimed to have invented jazz. His first jazz com position, "New Orleans Blues," was written in 1902. Morton was King of Jazz in the 1920s but fell into hard times and obscurity during the Depression. He died in 1941.

Although her cousin, Leontyne Price, is known as a great opera star, Dionne Warwick, whose niece is Whitney Houston and who is best known for her 66 popular albums, also sings opera. She has performed with Placido Domino and Jose Carrerra.

For many years, the Apollo Theatre on 125th Street in Harlem, New York, was the only major showcase for black talent in the United States. Performers such as Ella Fitzgerald, James Brown, Luther Vandross and Stephanie Mills scored their first successes on Amateur Night at the Apollo.

Charley Pride, the first successful African-American country music star who won a Grammy in 1972, began his career singing between innings of a company-sponsored baseball game where he was a player.

The New Negro Theater was founded in Los Angeles, California in 1939 by Langston Hughes. Their first performance was Hughes's play *Don't You want to Be Free?* Langston Hughes, considered one of the most important African-American writers of the 20th century was dubbed the poet laureate of the Negro race in 1960.

The television miniseries *Roots* won nine Emmy Awards in 1977, including one for Quincy Jones for outstanding achievement in musical composition.

Although he had written and performed many rock 'n' roll classics like "Johnny B. Goode," "Roll Over Beethoven" and "Reelin' and Rockin'," Chuck Berry's first number one *Billboard* single was "My Ding-a-Ling" in October of 1972.

Johnny Mathis, born in 1935 in San Francisco, obtained more than 50 gold and platinum records. His album *Johnny's Greatest Hits* was on the *Billboard* Top Album Charts for 490 continuous weeks, a Guiness Record.

The first Academy Award nomination for an African-American actress went to Dorothy Dandridge for her role in *Carmen Jones*. She lost the award to Grace Kelly. Dandridge's first movie role was a bit part in the 1937 Marx Brothers comedy, *A Day at the Races*.

In 1999, Indianapolis honored native Kenneth "Babyface" Edmonds by naming a 25-mile stretch of Interstate route 65 the Kenneth "Babyface" Edmonds Highway. This is the first time that a living African-American received such an honor in Indiana.

Noble Sissle and Eubie Blake composed the musical score of the review *Shuffle Along*, which opened on Broadway in 1921. One of the songs, "I'm Just Wild About Harry," was used years later for Harry Truman's presidential campaign.

Arthur Mitchell was the first male recipient of a dance award from the New York City High School of Performing Arts in 1951. He became the first African-American principal artist with the New York City Ballet in 1956, and founded the Dance Theatre of Harlem.

In 1984, Wynton Marsalis, a 22-year-old African American trumpet prodigy, was the first person in the history of the Grammys to win awards in both jazz and classical categories.

Lena Horne was born in Brooklyn, New York, in 1917, and began her career at the age of 16 as a chorus girl at the Cotton Club in Harlem. A Hollywood star in the 1940s, she was the pin-up girl for African-American soldiers during World War II. She was the first African-American actress to be given a long-term contract with a major film studio, MGM.

Alvin Ailey's American Dance Theater Company, founded in 1958, was the first black modern dance troupe to perform in the Metropolitan Opera House in New York.

Dubbed the "Black Martha Stewart," B. Smith, former model (she was the first African-American woman to appear on the cover of *Mademoiselle*) and restaurateur hosts a nationally-syndicated TV show featuring home, garden, health, and beauty. In addition she has created a new lifestyle magazine, *B. Smith Style Magazine*.